Daddy

Something to
hold you over
till great-escape
fall 2001-Love
you always
Joni

Peace Like a River

REFRESHING YOUR SOUL IN QUIET PLACES

DONNY FINLEY

Harvest House Publishers
EUGENE, OREGON

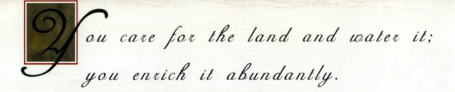

You care for the land and water it;
you enrich it abundantly.

The streams of God are filled with water
to provide the people with grain,
for so you have ordained it.

The Book of Psalms

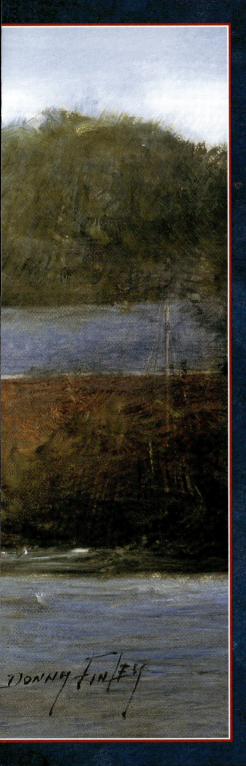

Donny Finley

Still glides the Stream, and shall for ever glide...
WILLIAM WORDSWORTH

The Lord is my shepherd, I shall not be in want.
He makes me lie down in green pastures,
he leads me beside quiet waters...
THE BOOK OF PSALMS

Oh river, gentle river! gliding on
In silence underneath this starless sky!
Thine is a ministry that never rests
Even while in living slumber.

WILLIAM CULLEN BRYANT

River

Never did sun more beautifully steep
In his first splendor, valley, rock, or hill;
Ne'er saw I, never felt, a calm so deep!
The river glideth at his own sweet will...
WILLIAM WORDSWORTH

5

Roads

Rivers are roads that move and carry us
whither we wish to go.

PASCAL

There is a river whose streams make glad
the city of God, the holy place
where the Most High dwells.

THE BOOK OF PSALMS

Dwelling

See the rivers, how they run,
Changeless to the changeless sea.

CHARLES KINGSLEY

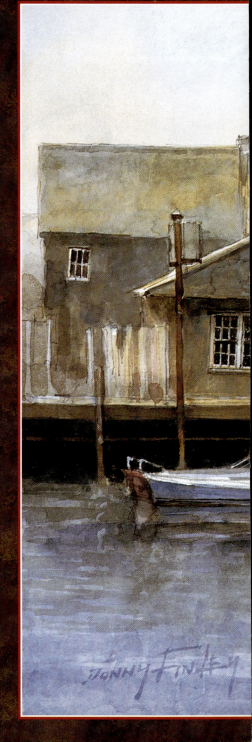

Two ways the rivers
Leap down to different seas,
   and as they roll
Grow deep and still,
   and their majestic presence
Becomes a benefaction
   to the towns
They visit, wandering
   silently among them,
Like patriarchs old among
   their shining tents.

LONGFELLOW

How beautiful the water is!
To me 'tis wondrous fair–
No spot can ever lonely be
If water sparkle there;
It hath a thousand tongues of mirth,
Of grandeur, or delight,
And every heart is gladder made
When water greets the sight.

MRS. E. OAKES SMITH

Be it mine to draw from wisdom's fount,
pure as it flows, that calm of soul
which virtue only knows.
AESCHYLUS

Let the sea resound, and everything in it,
the world, and all who live in it.
Let the rivers clap their hands...
THE BOOK OF PSALMS

Souls

The soul of the river had entered my soul,
And the gathered power of my soul was moving
So swiftly, it seemed to be at rest
Under cities of clouds and under
Spheres of silver and changing worlds...
EDGAR LEE MASTERS

The world turns softly

Not to spill its lakes and rivers,

The water is held in its arms

And the sky is held in the water.

What is water,

That pours silver,

And can hold the sky?

HILDA CONKLING, "WATER"

Lakes

They will neither hunger nor thirst, nor will the desert heat or the sun beat upon them. He who has compassion on them will guide them and lead them beside springs of water.

THE BOOK OF ISAIAH

Quiet

As the deer pants for streams of water,
so my soul pants for you, O God.

THE BOOK OF PSALMS

Give me my scallop-shell of quiet...

SIR WALTER RALEIGH

Waters

Ho, every one that thirsteth,
come ye to the waters...

THE BOOK OF ISAIAH

Shade

A little stream best fits a little boat...
ROBERT HERRICK

And see the rivers how they run
Through woods and meads, in shade and sun,

Sometimes swift, sometimes slow—
Wave succeeding wave, they go...

JOHN DYER

Sleeping

Very hot and still the air way,
Very smooth the gliding river,
Motionless the sleeping shadows.
LONGFELLOW, "HIAWATHA"

A voice of greeting from the wind was sent;
The mists enfolded me with soft white arms;
The birds did sing to lap me in content,
The rivers wove their charms—
And every little daisy in the grass
Did look up in my face, and smile to see me pass!

R.H. STODDARD

As Rivers Run

The voices of the subterranean river in the shadows
were different from the voices of the sunlit river
ahead. In the shadows against the cliff the river
was deep and engaged in profundities, circling back
on itself now and then to say things over to be sure
it had understood itself. But the river ahead came
out into the sunny world like a chatterbox, doing
its best to be friendly. It bowed to one shore and
then to the other so nothing would feel neglected.

NORMAN MACLEAN, *A River Runs Through It*

Fruit trees of all kinds will grow
on both banks of the river.
THE BOOK OF EZEKIEL

I chatter, chatter, as I flow
To join the brimming river,
For men may come and men may go,
But I go on forever.

TENNYSON, "THE BROOK"

Flow

Like a river glorious is God's perfect peace,
Over all victorious in its bright increase;
Perfect, yet it floweth fuller every day,
Perfect, yet it groweth deeper all the way.
Stayed upon Jehovah, hearts are fully blest;
Finding, as He promised, perfect peace and rest.
FRANCES R. HAVERGAL

All the rivers run into the

THE BOOK OF ECCLESIASTES

sea; yet the sea is not full.

Pebbles

O lovely eyes of azure,
Clear as the waters of a brook that run
Limpid and laughing in the summer sun!

LONGFELLOW

In the bed of the river there were pebbles and boulders, dry and white in the sun, and the water was clear and swiftly moving and blue in the channels...

ERNEST HEMINGWAY

Boulders

The winds with wonder whist,
Smoothly the waters kisst.

MILTON

A noise like of a hidden brook
In the leafy month of June,
That to the sleeping woods all night
Singeth a quiet tune.

CODERIDGE

See, how the stream has overflowed

Its banks, and o'er the meadow road

Is spreading far and wide!

LONGFELLOW

Woods

Rapaciously we gathered flowery spoils
From land and water; lilies of each hue—
Golden and white, that float upon the waves,
And court the wind.

WILLIAM WORDSWORTH

Springs

It was you who opened up springs and streams…
THE BOOK OF PSALMS

By shallow waters, to whose falls,
Melodious birds sing madrigals.
MARLOWE

 love any discourse of rivers, and fish and fishing.

IZAAK WALTON

Streams

'Tis Noon—a calm, unbroken sleep
Is on the blue waves of the deep;
A soft haze, like a fairy dream,
Is floating over wood and stream;
And many a broad magnolia flower
Within its shadowy woodland bower,
Is gleaming like a lovely star.
GEO. D. PRENTICE

Cool

Next we slid into the river and had a swim, so as to freshen up and cool off; then we set down on the sandy bottom where the water was about knee deep, and watched the daylight come. Not a sound anywheres—perfectly still—just like the whole world was asleep, only sometimes the bullfrogs a-cluttering, maybe...and you see the mist curl up off of the water, and the east reddens up, and the river, and you make out a log-cabin in the edge of the woods, away on the bank on t'other side of the river...then the nice breeze springs up, and comes fanning you from over there, so cool and fresh and sweet to smell on account of the woods and the flowers.

MARK TWAIN, *Huckleberry Finn*

Fresh

Deep

And liquid lapse of murmuring streams.
MILTON, *Paradise Lost*

mooth runs the water where the
brook is deep.

SHAKESPEARE

Brooks

He sendeth the springs into the rivers:
which run among the hills.
PRAYER BOOK

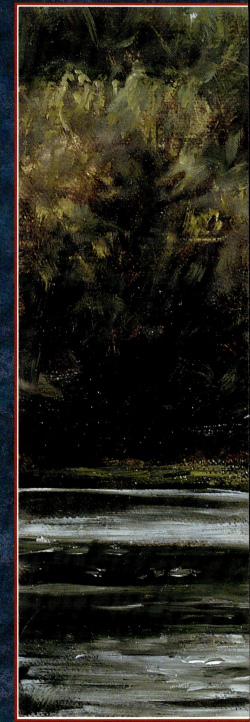

*The music of the brook silenced
all conversation.*
LONGFELLOW

Thou hastenest down between the hills

to meet me at the road,

The secret scarcely lisping of thy beautiful abode

Among the pines and mosses of yonder

shadowy height,

Where thou dost sparkle into song,

and fill the woods with light.

LUCY LARCOM, "FRIEND BROOK"

Heights

*He is like a tree planted by streams of water,
which yields its fruit in season
and whose leaf does not wither.*
THE BOOK OF PSALMS

The great waterfall pours down. . .

Caldron Pool is the big pool right under the cliffs at the western end of Narnia. The great waterfall pours down into it with a noise like everlasting thunder, and the River of Narnia flows out on the other side. The waterfall keeps the Pool always dancing and bubbling and churning round and round as if it were on the boil, and that of course is how it got its name of Caldron Pool. It is liveliest in the early spring when the waterfall is swollen with all the snow that has melted off the mountains from up beyond Narnia in the Western Wild from which the river comes.

C.S. LEWIS, *The Last Battle*

. . .with a noise like everlasting thunder.

I will give unto him that is athirst of the fountain
of the water of life freely.
THE BOOK OF REVELATION

I will extend peace to her like a river...
THE BOOK OF ISAIAH

He will be like a tree planted by the water
that sends out its roots by the stream.
It does not fear when heat comes;
its leaves are always green.
It has no worries in a year of drought
and never fails to bear fruit.

THE BOOK OF JEREMIAH

Sweet are the little brooks that run
O'er pebbles glancing in the sun,
Singing in soothing tunes.

HOOD, "TOWN AND COUNTRY"

And nearer to the river's
    trembling edge
There grew broad flag-flowers,
    purple, pranked with white,
And starry river buds
    among the sedge,
And floating water-lilies,
    broad and bright.

SHELLEY

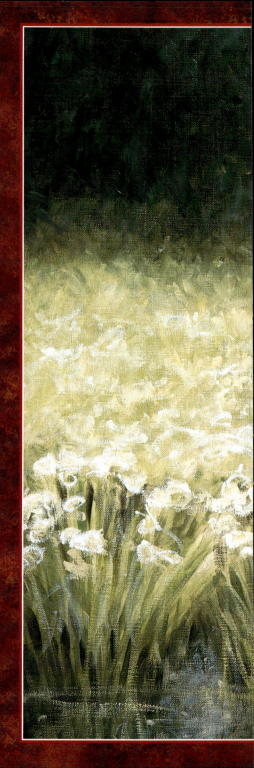

Silver

Now at the close of this soft summer's day,
Inclined upon the river's flowery side,
I pause to see the sportive fishes play,
And cut with finny oars the sparkling tide.

VALDARNE

A spring there is, whose silver waters show
Clear as a glass the shining sands below...

POPE

Sands

Full many a glorious morning have I seen
Flatter the mountain-tops with sovereign eye,
Kissing with golden face the meadows green,
Gilding pale streams with heavenly alchemy.

SHAKESPEARE

He lieth under the shady trees,
  in the covert of the reed, and fens.
The shady trees cover him with their shadow;
  the willows of the brook compass him about.
Behold, he drinketh up a river, and hastest not.

THE BOOK OF PROVERBS

My people will live in peaceful dwelling places; in secure homes, in undisturbed places of rest.

THE BOOK OF ISAIAH

Rest

There was a time when meadow, grove, and stream,
The earth, and every common sight,
To me did seem
Appareled in celestial light,
The glory and the freshness of a dream.

WILLIAM WORDSWORTH

There is no small pleasure in sweet water.

OVID